"This collection is a lavish feast
through the rugged and often p(
relations, and the effect of politi
of these poems are also about food. So much delicious food. Ramadan's
gift with words and story made me want to eat the pages. A tender and
rich debut collection by a brilliant young writer."
—SUZETTE MAYR

"From Canadian coastal rains and prairie winters to the sand and seas
of Bierut and Khor Fakkan, *This Sweet Rupture* emulates the warmth of
each kitchen, mosque, or picnic, whether in a Dairy Queen parking lot
or sandy beach. Heartwarming and heartbreaking conversations with
family and fathers that yearn to shelter a sense of safety. Ramadan
playfully reframes ignorance across each stanza through juxtapositions
between Islamophobic encounters and things like McDonald's removal
of chocolate vanilla twist ice cream. These are haunting and humorous
lessons in how to be human. Each poem is a whole world of love amongst
our world of wars. Sugars and spices become portals, unravelling
histories of manmade violence."
—KAITYLN PURCELL, author of *ʔbédayine*

"*This Sweet Rupture* is waves hushing Vancouver and frost heaves
drowning prairies; a tidal force punctuated by cassette tapes and six-
seater sedans. Ramadan layers sonic patterns into sensory delights
around the dinner table: an Oreo McFlurry, a bowl of lentil soup, a poetic
conjuring of stories stuck between fathers and sons that find their way
out in the swirl of sugared hot tea. A dazzling collection that makes room
for memories of war that not even The Big One can wipe out."
—CRISTALLE SMITH, author of *Invisible Lives*

"Omar Ramadan's *This Sweet Rupture* traces the minutiae of vulnerability,
the texture of identity, and the redolence of memory amid the spectres
of human cruelty. In urgent and tender language, Omar reminds us that,
though the echoes, scars, and shadows of war surround us, we can draw
strength from family love and the abiding power of beauty in community."
—UCHECHUKWU PETER UMEZURIKE, author of *there's more*

**THIS
SWEET
RUPTURE**

THIS SWEET RUPTURE

OMAR RAMADAN

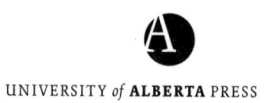

UNIVERSITY *of* ALBERTA PRESS

Published by

University of Alberta Press
1-16 Rutherford Library South
11204 89 Avenue NW
Edmonton, Alberta, Canada T6G 2J4
amiskwaciwâskahikan | Treaty 6 |
Métis Territory
ualbertapress.ca | uapress@ualberta.ca

Copyright © 2025 Omar Ramadan

LIBRARY AND ARCHIVES CANADA
CATALOGUING IN PUBLICATION

Title: This sweet rupture / Omar Ramadan.
Names: Ramadan, Omar (Lebanese-Canadian writer), author.
Series: Robert Kroetsch series.
Description: Series statement: Robert Kroetsch series
Identifiers: Canadiana (print) 2024048195X | Canadiana (ebook) 20240481968 | ISBN 9781772127973 (softcover) | ISBN 9781772128154 (PDF) | ISBN 9781772128147 (EPUB)
Classification: LCC PS8635.A46137 T45 2025 | DDC C811/.6—dc23

First edition, first printing, 2025.
First printed and bound in Canada by Houghton Boston Printers, Saskatoon, Saskatchewan.
Editing by Kimmy Beach.
Proofreading by Jim Johnstone.

A volume in the Robert Kroetsch Series.

All rights reserved. No part of this publication may be produced, stored in a retrieval system, or transmitted in any form or by any means (electronic, mechanical, photocopying, recording, generative artificial intelligence [AI] training, or otherwise) without prior written consent. Contact University of Alberta Press for further details.

University of Alberta Press supports copyright. Copyright fuels creativity, encourages diverse voices, promotes free speech, and creates a vibrant culture. Thank you for buying an authorized edition of this book and for complying with the copyright laws by not reproducing, scanning, or distributing any part of it in any form without permission. You are supporting writers and allowing University of Alberta Press to continue to publish books for every reader.

University of Alberta Press is committed to protecting our natural environment. As part of our efforts, this book is printed on Enviro Paper: it contains 100% post-consumer recycled fibres and is acid- and chlorine-free.

GPSR: Easy Access System Europe | Mustamäe tee 50, 10621 Tallinn, Estonia | gpsr.requests@easproject.com

University of Alberta Press gratefully acknowledges the support received for its publishing program from the Government of Canada, the Canada Council for the Arts, and the Government of Alberta through the Alberta Media Fund.

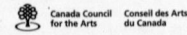

For my father

Contents

I

2   Shorbet Adas is Served at the IIC Daily Iftar
4   ذيحة or قربان or Your First Beheading Video—Part I
5   "What Am I Slaughtering Myself For?"
6   "How Old Were You When 9/11 Happened?" or "Do You Even Remember That Day?"
7   When Al Jazeera Newscasters Stopped Speaking, Circa 2004
9   and the state can't wait to rapture us
10   Love Poem to a Car
12   One Militia Man
14   Klash Joins Us at the Dinner Table
15   Lebanese Zaatar Mix

II

18   This Sweet Rupture
20   White Out
25   Cloud Seeding the Empty Quarter
27   For the Syrian Oud Player
28   Suckers بالساحة
32   Dogs Myth-Make the Desert

III

42   Basha Sparrows
43   God Lives in the Gap Between a Horse's Ears
45   نار ورمان
47   Sesame Love
49   Death Attends the عزاء
50   We Stop to Imagine a Skyline Without the Fire Stack
51   Cosmo? Or Lessons in Cultural Un-Communication
53   Origin Myths or A Poem for Survivor's Guilt—Cut Up
54   ذيحة or قربان or Your First Beheading Video—Part II
56   Immigrant Father Horticulture

57   *Acknowledgements*

لو كنت من مازن لم تستبح ابلي
—QURAIT BIN ANEEF AL-TAMIMI

I had no words. *Come, let us go home Little Father. When you are of age you shall find the words*, he said. *But always be careful—to hunt a word is to hunt a life.*
—MUKOMA WA NGUGI

I

Shorbet Adas is Served at the IIC Daily Iftar

on Kingsway, amber streetlamps illuminate slick sleet sidewalk,
when maghrib is at four thirty, Vancouver
turned BC interior ghost town
except for the odd passerby, umbrella in hand,
raincoat tucked up to red ears, and
sex workers staging the street

> *One woman propositioned me once.*
> *I mentioned this was a mosque—*
> *she apologized and went on her way;*
> *no business here.*

My father parks the Mazda MPV   somewhere
we shuffle down creaking wood steps, wrapped in thrifted raincoats, boots,
air scented sandalwood bakhoor soaks into hair, skin.
We sit on carpeted floor   that loses bounce when IIC rebrands—
we break fast on Saudi dates, chunky lentil soup   after athan is called
in Styrofoam bowls
          while uncles wax politics   openly.

Someone snaps photos on a Kodak for the newsletter,
close-ups of faces, men huddled around food, spoons stuck in mouths
printed in black and white   digital comes soon after,

my father's good about keeping records:
          VHS > CDs > USBs > external hard drives > SSDs
          backups to backups to backups   *just in case—*

The evening rain stops on the ride home
where the radio host speaks of The Big One
that'll wash away the island, Vancouver,
swallow us all into the dark Pacific
bodies of water meet body of water;

in school we're taught to run for higher ground if it ever happens,
I wonder if the gym roof is high enough.

they've been talking about that forever,
it'll be forever before it comes.

The cassette whirs in the cassette player
the qari recites a surah I have trouble remembering
rain returns as we cross the Portmann or the Patullo;
all bridges lead to:
tomorrow we'll eat lentil soup,
tomorrow we'll hear about The Big One

ذبيحة or قربان or Your First Beheading Video—Part I

if you squint hard enough,
you can trick your eyes into believing
pools of blood soaking earth
spilled paint
meant for canvas

"What Am I Slaughtering Myself For?"

And your eyes are rivers
saffron stained and dripping
flavours only home could hold.

This water—salted liver hand-
delivered in a gilded gold casket
leaves us suspended in stainless steel

tea pots blackened in fire.
Gas stovetop, raging blue flame
midday sun heat singes onion flesh

caramel brown.
At this dinner table let there be
a criss-cross of arms

a highway of fingers making waves
raise edges softer than razor blades.
You toil until your feet turn

stone.
Now, silver hair slips from your head
caught in the Dyson or in our mouths

until our stomachs fill.

"How Old Were You When 9/11 Happened?" or "Do You Even Remember That Day?"

i.
McDonald's no longer serves
chocolate vanilla twist ice cream
sometimes Oreo McFlurries
mostly broken machines.

ii.
the neighbourhood erupts
screeching bottle rockets pepper
the sky when it's darkest
just before the dawn.

iii.
boys linger in the rear
waiting for the imam to enter ruku'u—
join congregation
at the right moment.

iv.
the pamphlet in the mailbox asks
have you accepted our lord and saviour jesus christ?
The pamphlet from the mailbox
finds itself in the recycling bin.

v.
invasion anxiety arrives in the gap
between the door and the frame
in the form of ants seeking sugar—
we learn to live with it.

vi.
a hole from a pellet gun in the kitchen window
screams neighbourly hate—
we learn to turn other cheeks,
we learn to live with it.

When Al Jazeera Newscasters Stopped Speaking, Circa 2004

The sun refused to give warmth,
it hovered low
in an evening sky made of blood and oil.
It, a large pool,
swallowed by a horizon of sand and black ash
that my eyes could only see through a CRT TV
sitting comfortably
wearing a bleach-white doily on its head,
nestled between family photos,
a mosaic of chewed-through wires, books
clutching dust as though it were relic.

Here, I listened
to the endless falling of a knife
gliding through onion flesh
forcing from the crevasses
avalanches of tears
not meant for onions.

Here, the sun died on a pixelated plate.
The world stopped revolving
air turned mercury
threatening to drown our lungs
and a moment
turned into a year
as the clock quit.

I was never taught how to pull tears from wells.
I never knew that buckets could be heavy
that they threaten to pull you in.
I never thought loved ones could turn into specks, molecules, atoms,
scattered to desert winds.

Our martyrs aren't celebrated here.
Their names pass from lips
to lips
until they're chafed from whispers
and the living room is left littered with memories.

and the state can't wait to rapture us

over Whatsapp video
my father holds three passports
in the palm of his safe.
He says, it's just in case, you never know
when you'll need it,
when you'll need
safety.

I say, you're in the most
turbulent place on earth,
there is only trouble there.
He says, you don't understand trouble
you don't get turbulence
you don't know when safety
will dry up.

He pushes me to get other passports
he says, you can hide them in the bottom of your safe
I say, I don't have one
he says, under the mattress is fine
I say, I'm not a dragon   I'm not gonna
curl up on top of my mattress
every night
dream of safety in pages
dream of peace in
gaps between faded stamps.

My father says, تصطفل
when the time comes,
don't come crying
I'll tell you I told you so.

End call.

Love Poem to a Car

Bil-Dahye El-Janoobiye, the forty-year-old olive oil green Mercedes
nestles in the shade of my grandparents' apartment block
—across from a graffitied garage door stating: mawqef Abu Amir; kis emo
le byo2f—
facades scarred by civil war ended yesterday.

We pile into the backseat, the six-seater sedan holds double on a good day,
my grandparents sit in the front, my mother wedged between them,
the scent of old leather, sandalwood, cigarettes, coffee, gunpowder
linger regardless of how many times it's—

يعطيك العافية يا عم

The forty-year-old olive oil green Mercedes winds
through narrow streets like a snake dodging scar-faced walls
plastered in campaign posters from past elections, ongoing elections,
future elections, and my grandfather
lays on the horn—

يعطيك العافية يا عم

The Mercedes joins
the flow of morning Beiruty traffic,
its windows down because the AC doesn't work,
its windows down because the radio doesn't sing, and
I wonder if she did, would she serenade us with music
or stories of how this car used to carry German, Italian, Spanish tourists
or how it climbed Lebanese mountains
escaping to safe havens,
and we take in the sounds of streets, the vendors selling-yelling
عالسكين يا بطيخ
عل بطاطا عل بطاطا
كلينكس كلينكس

while my grandfather chain smokes, cracks jokes,
curses the mothers, the brothers, the sisters, the ancestors
of every pedestrian and driver on the—

يعطيك العافية يا عم

We scramble out of the car
and watch my grandfather drive off in search of parking
to smoke more cigarettes
and the ocean spurned by the wind hits the seawall
and the Mercedes
is doused in sea salt and shell shards
and it ducks and weaves
escaping the spray of ten thousand more waves.

And I feel the cool summer breeze on my face
as we return home
the sun sinks into the Mediterranean
an invisible moon climbs over the horizon
and all of us packed into the forty-year-old olive oil green Mercedes
which protests as it climbs hills
crawls through military checkpoints
where men draped in the olive oil green of war
with M16s darker than coffee grounds
they stare us down
their eyelids never close as the brakes struggle
to stop the car from—

يعطيك العافية يا عم

الله يعافيك

One Militia Man

Stands on a street corner
Sometime in the 1980s

His finger hovers over the trigger
Of his army-issue
Russian-made
AK-47

He's surrounded by sandbags
Empty shells and sniper fire
      (that would find its way into his left foot
            now one foot is half an inch smaller than the other)

A camo-green helmet hides
The start of a curly afro
Aviator sunglasses conceal
Hazel eyes
His military jacket unbuttoned
The sleeves rolled all the way to his elbows
And beneath it all
A green T-shirt
      (which I used to sleep in)
With an orange tiger prowls
Its fangs bared and inscribed:
Take No Prisoners.

We walk the streets of Beirut with the militia man—

Down this street
I raced tanks with a friend.

On that rooftop
I killed a man.

I used to have a car like that
Before it erupted in flames.

Over there I learned that I went blind in one eye—

And we stop at a corner
Littered with cigarette butts, empty plastic bags,
And beggars asking
For a little
While dusty sandbags sit against curbs
We wander streets
Surrounded by walls, towering buildings
Peppered in bullet wounds,
                              And crowds and the wailing gulls

Klash Joins Us at the Dinner Table

We are called away from watching Dexter's Lab
        from sitting cross-legged on marble
        playing mancala Monopoly
        until the bones in our legs numb;
we sit
gawk at the meal
gift-wrapped in a blanket perfumed in metal and gunpowder.

My father hovers over us
unveils Klash
as though he were a magician
pulling a card from his sleeve
        setting a dove free—

He cradles the rifle in his arms
        stresses it's not a toy, keep fingers
        away from the trigger before

he decapitates the rifle
 pulls its body apart
   lays its carcass at our hands;
  we learn to keep childhood
   in the gaps between bullets
    scattered on the dinner table
     the small space where trigger lives
    in between iron sights
     where you'd look through
       devouring another man whole.

Lebanese Zaatar Mix

i.
At the bottom of the freezer,
entombed in a black plastic bag entombed in a Ziploc bag
beneath chicken, freezer-burned

> [which mama tells me isn't a thing.
> Yet I see the twisted, churned, flesh
> as though the bird had come back to life
> then died again]

is the زعتر.

> ii.
> هون أنا
> شبكتي برمي كنت
> العصافير بسطاد كنت
> الليل بعتمة بنام كنت
> كتابي و بارودتي معي

iii.
The black grocery bag[s]

> [my grandmothers fill with لوز أخضر and جنارك
> and موز and loose leaf
> and حصرم and ورق عنب
> childhood that weighs as much as salt stock in Beirut's port]

absorbs زعتر and homeland
located in photographs and stories
in between plastic fibres of its body;

I try not to devour.

15

iv.
In the hills, زعتر grows long, wild, hairlike.
We hike mountains of rock and thorn
that jabs, pokes our exposed flesh.
Our blood mixes with red earth.
My grandfather walks ahead
pulls stalk after stalk.

Thyme falls through his fingers,
scatters in the wind,
turns the mountain زعتر
ready for غربة
not yet frozen.

II

This Sweet Rupture

i.
My father still tells the same joke
when my mother sips
Lipton Yellow Label black tea, calls it
bitter
from her favourite فنجان
the ones she bought in a set of six:

اصبعك اغمس
you're sweet enough.

ii.
I try to find my grandfather's house بالبقاع
on Google Maps.
The yellow figure hangs from my mouse's cursor
hovering over the un-highlighted road
before flying back to the corner of my screen.

Google tells me
the roads here are not worth the memory.

iii.
The WhatsApp family group chat dings
at three in the morning.
I flit through a deluge of messages and
filtered photos of long lost family;

sweetness knows no time zones.

iv.
I pour orange blossom extract into the
sugar-water mixture simmering on the stovetop.
The kitchen turns into a baklawa orchard
waiting to be soaked.

v.

I give up on Google Maps
I fly home to my family photos and find the house.
I land on the marble-stone steps.
We eat breakfast, pour شاي بالفناجين
My grandfather asks for سكر,
asks for another
for more
until his tea is more sugar than tea.
My dad makes the same joke before it dissolves in the cup.
I look at the time and

vi.

علبة السكر فاضية
The steeped Lipton Yellow Label black tea goes
cold
as I search for the last granules in the cabinet.
I ask my mom if there's any sugar left.

اصبعك اغمس
You're sweet enough.

White Out
For Marc L.

We arrive in a place known as Virden, Manitoba, late in the night, the ice storm chased us, nipped at our heels, all the way from the outskirts of Regina where we passed overturned sixteen wheelers, their cargo spread out on the road like pulled guts of fish, dissipated, replaced by the beginnings of a blizzard. Snowflakes stream past the windshield, the headlights of my car illuminate a gate blocking the Trans-Canada Highway stretching out ahead of us, amber lights affixed atop the gate flash at us, and the "Road Closed" sign bars us from continuing.

"Now what? Do we stay the night?" I ask my friend who I picked up in Calgary, the glow from his phone illuminates his face, I can't tell if he's stressed about the road closure or the blizzard bearing down, but the dark bags under his eyes tell me he is tired.

"There's a Comfort Inn just behind us. We could get a room and wait it out," he replies.

"We could," I reply. Waiting it out was the best option after crawling across the prairie highway east of Regina, hoping we didn't end up in a ditch, or crashed into another car, I pray silently, my breath caught in my throat, every time the wheels lost grip, and the car slipped on patches of invisible ice dotting the asphalt.

We turn away from the barricades, and head to the A&W parking lot. One plaza over, the hotel looms over the fast-food joint, and in the darkness, in the low light, my mind's eye plays tricks, the three-level building is gargantuan, made of cement, glass windows upon glass windows, it eclipses the smaller buildings around us, like it had been someone's vanity project.

"How much? Three hundred dollars? For the night?" My friend's on the phone with someone from the hotel, and he blurts out the going rate. My heart pounds in my chest. Whoever manned the desk that night must have been given the green light to increase the prices of rooms due to the highway closure, but it was scummy. There is no way we could sleep in the car, we had no sleeping bags, and with the weather turning, we'd freeze to death.

"I'm not paying that."

"Well, shit, neither am I. That's crazy money."

"Should we keep going then?"

"If there's another way, yeah."

"Maybe we should get some food or something." I gesture to the A&W, the car bathes in the orange and white neon sign. My friend agrees, and he steps out of the car onto the slick pavement.

"Hey, I could *skate* on this." There's a palpable excitement in his voice, boyish, I forgot my skates in a Browns Shoes disposable bag back in Edmonton, I see it in my mind's eye, stuffed away in storage collecting dust. I look through Google Maps for an alternative route while he laces up in the back seat, a drift of cold air sails through the car, my friend takes off on iced pavement, skates circles and figure eights. I watch in disbelief while filming, I make sure the camera's steady, but all I want to do is watch my friend skate in a parking lot.

We're greeted by the smell of grease inside the empty A&W, and a look of surprise on the employee's face. She stands behind the cash, smiling, I don't see anyone else there, and assume she's the only one working the joint that night. Ice rain, blizzard, heat wave, the only thing that could stop a 24/7 A&W from functioning is a power outage.

"Do you know if there are any back roads that can get us around the road closure? We're trying to get to Winnipeg." my friend says.

"Ah? Hold on." She walks into the back and drags out another employee from the kitchen. He stands there, his hands on his hips, head cocked to one side, studying us.

"You want to know if there's a way around?" We nod. "I know these roads, but I'm not going to tell you. I don't recommend going through them if you don't know. If you break down, if you end up in a ditch, there won't be anyone that can come save you, not in this weather. Stay the night instead." The warning feels like a cliché from an 80s horror flick: "old man warns teens not to go into forest; teens all die."

And we follow the trope.

Our friend in Winnipeg calls and confirms an open route south of Virden, south of the Trans-Canada Highway, that would get us to Brandon, where we can stay the night for a much more reasonable hundred and fifty bucks at The Day's Inn. My friend books the room as we're heading out, I pat the dash, and say, "yallah" under my breath encouraging the car to take the brunt of the storm.

The lights of Virden fade in the rear-view mirror, the blizzard swallows the town whole. The road ahead of us is thick with snow, I peer out the windshield, but it's as though someone draped a white sheet over the glass. In the side mirrors, I see the tires kick up snow, the rear red taillights illuminate the flying specks.

"Check out the snow in the mirrors. Looks like sparks," I say.

"Oh, holy, yeah. I might have to use this image for my writing," my friend replies.

"It's a pretty good image."

"Surreal. Really does look like we're on fire."

We talk about writing, music, food, anything to distract us from the weather. There are breaks in the storm, we find respite by homes entrenched behind four walls of trees, I assume the trees help block the blizzard since we're no longer swaying around the road. But, as soon as we get past the entrenched plots of land, the blizzard starts again.

I fiddle with the lights looking for the fog lights, instead, I switch them off, the white sheet turns into a blindfold, the darkness engulfing us felt like we'd been stuffed into an oil lamp and thrown off the bow of a boat into the deepest waters. My heart catches in my throat, and I slow down, figure out the knobs. The fog lights cut through the blizzard illuminating the shoulder of the road.

"I'm going to need some help navigating," I say.

"Sure, what can I do?"

"If you can just let me know every little bit how close I am to the shoulder, that would be great."

"I can do that." He presses his face against the passenger side window, I lean forward against the steering wheel, my grip stretches my knuckles taut against my skin. I feel the car drift, the blizzard pulls and pushes the car in the direction it blows, and I try adjusting on my own.

"How's it looking over there?"

"You're good," he replies. We carry on with this game, the blizzard drifts us, I adjust hoping I did a good job, he tells me I did a good job, or if I'm nearing the shoulder, or if I'm over the line, until we see lights from oncoming vehicles appear through the billowing snow. I slow down, give a wide berth, and I'm sure the people in the trucks have the same questions about us as we do about them, namely, where are you going? And why did you choose to go out in *this* weather? But we don't stop to exchange pleasantries, I can't see into their cabins, and they can't see into ours. Their red taillights fade in the storm.

We arrive in Souris, Manitoba, somewhere south, somewhere along the Red Coat Trail, trees dot the community, protect the buildings from the blizzard. We travel down Main Street, through the middle of town, we pass a herd of deer sheltering from the storm. Their eyes glint in the car's headlights, their necks crane over their shoulders and they stare.

We travel through Souris, the community is sheltered away in their homes, except for one person in an Anytime Fitness, who we see running on a treadmill through the front window.

We carry on, the blizzard moving west, us northeast. The road opens up, snowdrifts from the blizzard line the shoulders, they remind me of sand drifts on rural desert roads back home.

I plow into the shoulder, climb over snowdrifts, powder flies up around us. We bomb down the road through the aftermath, we keep an eye on the shoulders, watch for glinting eyes.

Cloud Seeding the Empty Quarter

Arabian Gulf's sea water laps up Khor
Fakkan Beach dragging in empty soda
bottles, seashells, fish carcasses

       still thin flesh scaly
       skin hanging bones.

I'm told not to touch dead
fish along coastlines without
washing my hands after;

       the bacteria could kill me.

I opt for a charred pointed stick found
near remnants of a campfire to spear

       a fish in its dark eye gray-
       black putty beneath pressure.

My uncle spends evenings fishing
for sharks: we watch him cast
his fishing rod—raw chicken attached

       metal hook—pitches overhead,
       sends lines snapping, his arms lightning.

He pulls baby shark after baby shark, letting them go;
I wonder if it's the same shark bamboozled every time
getting caught in the trap meant for its sibling or another.

We eat cold chicken shawarma we bought from a restaurant—
       the ones where fridges hum, stocked with Coke, Fanta, ayran,
         intermix sounds of long knives slicing through meat
         and seagulls squawking in parking lots—

on the beach, our tent, near an open fire, listen
to rolling waves, silent hope we don't get food poisoning.

We don't

hear the cop car pull up
until doors slam
feet shuffle over sand.

My uncle scrambles out
of the tent, leaves the flap open in his wake.

The cops ask:

if we swam across the Gulf, if we're from Iran, if
we're illegal aliens until they're satisfied with my uncle's answers.
        I wonder how many bodies they've seen
        washed up alongside soda bottles, seashells, fish
        carcasses, bloated in seawater. If families on the other
        side wait for news or just assume their loved ones are dead.

My uncle tells us to sleep;
Tomorrow's a long day.

For the Syrian Oud Player

When we finally noticed the Arab spring fading, the earth
split open underneath our feet, the frigid winter air set
deep beneath our skin, we sang for revolutions that never turned.
Your music washed over foreign shores, littered with bodies
of those that could not swim.

A cabbie in Istanbul transports me from a street corner
I mispronounce, to another street corner
I mispronounce. They wade through traffic, like a swimmer wading
in shallows, dodging sea urchins, fish asking if you'd like to buy water—

I am deposited on the corner after depositing cash in the cabbie's hands.
I walk up water-streaked cobblestone streets. Enter through the red door,
take in the scent of boiling tea, fresh paperback books. Crumple into
a wood chair beneath stairs, wait for you to stroll in with a black case
strapped to your back, a quiver holding music.

And they say you will play music.
And they say you are from Damascus.
And they say you are from Aleppo.
And they say you are from Homs.
And they say you are from Latkia. And they say

you are from all the places my ancestors smashed rose petals
into jam, sealed in glass jars, wrapped in plastic, transported across
continents, oceans, settling into a childhood home
not yet shattered by grief.

The bookstore settles into silence. You cradle your oud on your knee.
You place the reeshe between your fingers. You strum, fill the space
with music, swallow the outside world
into abstract silence.

Suckers بالساحة

The first casualty of the night was the black and white patterned
كفية wrapped around my brother's neck, stripped away by a traffic cop
standing on the street corner beneath the glowing
yellow and green neon Subway sign.

The air hung heavy, humid. Windows and storefronts blurred with
condensation obscuring people in shops, consumers in the fast-food chain
munching on footlongs. For a time, my sister ordered vegetarian-only
sandwiches: lettuce, tomatoes, cucumbers, sweet onion dressing—a salad
encased in bread. I never understood why she wouldn't just make her own
at home. Would have been cheaper too.

I always asked her to turn it into a combo, so I could sneak
two double chocolate macadamia cookies and a Pepsi. The distance
between the apartment block where we lived, and the Subway
was فشختين; we always ordered delivery.

The traffic cop made us stop in front of him.
Asked us where we were headed, asked us why.
He pointed to the كفية, ordered it to come off my brother's neck.

He pointed to the red and white شماغ around mine, ordered it off
my neck. I hesitated. Looked around. This one belonged to my father and
was not mine to give nor was it his to take. I clutched the ends of the شماغ.
The fabric felt coarse against my skin. The smell of my father's perfume
lingered in the threads.

Traffic slowed around us. People stared out their cars before speeding
away. One pulled up behind us with its emergency lights flashing. The traffic
cop's face glowed amber. His fingers hovered over the شماغ. The كفية
tucked away under his arm. My father hopped out of the car and approached.

The traffic cop stuck his finger out at us: These your kids?
My father nodded.
The traffic cop gestured to the شماغ, to the كفية under his arm:
Can't let them have these tonight. Take them home.

My father nodded and the scarves were returned. We slipped
them into the back seat. My father drove away, and the traffic distracted
the traffic cop.

My brother and I marched on, شماغ-less, كفية-less. We rounded the corniche
passing beneath transplanted palm trees and grass patches. I slipped out of
my sandals. The grass sliced beneath my feet. A wayward soccer ball rolled
into my path, and I passed it back to kids wearing knock-off Real Madrid
and Barcelona jerseys with their names printed on the backs. The water
in the man-made lake lapped up and over onto the sidewalk, breaking free.

The sun dipped into the horizon. We picked up the pace. Others
passed us heading in the same direction, whispering among themselves. Some
wore the شماغ and the كفية. Some hid it under their shirts. The fabric poked out.

The whisper network said to meet at the مسجد after مغرب.

The whisper network said to come مستعدين. For anything.

I considered stopping for a doughnut. The Krispy Kreme was فشختين from the مسجد.
After every Eid prayer, a friend and I would ditch the congregation, sit at the
Krispy Kreme, listen to the خطيب over the speakers. The sermon paired
well with an original glazed.

I thought about the sugar melting on my tongue. I loved watching the doughnuts
from behind the glass pass through the conveyer, cooked fresh and live.
How the dough would glide into the oil, come out looking inflated. How the
inflated dough passed under endless sugar glaze. I always asked
for a fresh one straight from the conveyer.

I considered stopping for a doughnut, but my brother spurred us on,
and the crowd of شباب spurred us on,
and I didn't see my friend who said he'd be there.

Inside the مسجد, the cold air from the ever-going air conditioning
made my body ache. The imam sat in the centre beneath the grand
chandelier. On Fridays, during the sermons, I wondered what would
happen if the chandelier broke loose. How many people would be squished.
How thick the blood would run over the carpet.
I stood in the back of the crowd, away from the chandelier, the seated men.
The شباب remained outside. My brother linked with his friends, they joined
the congregation. A man stood at the door. His face concealed by a شماغ
wrapped around it.
A square shaped device bulged in his pocket. He moved out of the way
as I approached. I put my hand on the handle and pulled the grand door open.
Dense humid air swept inwards. I peeked through the crack at the شباب milling
around بالساحة. The man at the door put his hand on the handle,
pushed it closed.

جوا أو برا: لازم تختار

I stepped outside into the dense humid air. The imam's voice sounded over
speakers. The شباب بالساحة formed into rows linked arms
in arms chanting in unison:

بالروح بالدم نفديك يا غزة

بالروح بالدم نفديك يا غزة

بالروح بالدم نفديك يا غزة

I descended the marble staircase, my sandals in hand. The fine layer of
sand shrouding the steps found their way between my toes and covered my
feet. I slipped into my sandals and joined the شباب.

The chants grew louder, and the stomping vibrated the ground beneath us. We marched around the square arms interlinking arms. Made it ours. Made it chant. Made it move. Made it—

You never forget the sound of the baton colliding with the body. Like carpets being beat to get rid of dust or sand. Like the healthy heartbeat in a stethoscope, steady. Like the slamming of the car door—

The ساحة emptied. We scattered in the streets. The Krispy Kreme
blurred past me. The imam's voice over the speakers dimmed in the night.

I sprinted the long way home through back alleys beneath the moonlight. I missed the sharp grass beneath my feet. The smell of seawater lapping up onto sidewalk. The feeling of the humid air on my skin. The taste of sugar hanging on my tongue.

Dogs Myth-Make the Desert

November 4
6:00 a.m.

i.

        the American soldier living on the 25th floor

        dresses in desert camo

        rides the elevator

        to the third-floor parking lot

        in silence

        except today he hums

        the Star-Spangled Banner.

November 4
9:00 a.m.

ii.

a pack of dogs roams the deserted spaces beyond the gates, beyond the fences, covered in fleas, sand, mange. they make their homes in dune foxholes hunt jerboas, chickens, rats, food filled

dumpsters. they tell you not to approach black dogs, the ones with red eyes, the ones with fangs stretching down over their bottom lips, the ones that howl in the night. those can see jinn.

the black dogs travel with the white dogs with the brown dogs with the spotted dogs; they all see jinn.

November 4
11:00 a.m.

iii.

        for lunch, they serve lukewarm cheese pizza

        smothered in ketchup.

        flies circle above our heads

        diving at opportune moments,

        get sucked into sugar, melted cheese, oil,

        eat until they balloon

        explode in confetti of wings and blood.

November 4
12:45 p.m.

iv.

    the pack seeks shade beneath desert trees. god pours water into their shoe, leaves it out for them to share. god's footprints lead out into the desert. they kept one shoe on.

    the pack decides to war for water. their bodies fly in every direction their jaws snap in the air aiming for flesh attempting to draw blood. the shoe is knocked over, the desert drinks

    water, the desert drinks blood. the pack skulks away · licks its wounds   lives to fight itself
another day.

November 4
1:30 p.m.

v.

    the Arabic teacher never calls upon

    the expat kid with the broken grammar

    to test if he memorized the poem

    even though this time

    he memorized the poem:

    maybe if he was from Mazen

    the outcome would be different.

November 4
4:05 p.m.

vi.
        the pack reconciles sets out to find water
        to find God in a shoe in a public water
        fountain attached to a mosque abandoned
        to pigeons and geckos. the minaret lies on

        its side crumbled into ash, sand, dust. the
        pack guests God's home expel the geckos
        the pigeons set up a look out for jinn
        attempting infiltration in moonless

        nights their barking and howls echo long
        into morning winds join in sand twisters
        dance in deserted parking lots.

November 4
5:30 p.m.

vii.

    we ride the elevator to the second floor

    the soldier doesn't join us on our journey

    I imagine he's dug in a sand foxhole

    where a dog has urinated

    marking their territory their home

    desecrated

    by star-spangled boots.

November 4
8:30 p.m.

viii.

    the pack spends evenings praying to God in their own language. They pray for a good hunt for food for water for no more blood drunk desert for the jinn to leave them alone.

    tonight, jinn streak the sky leave trails in their wake   mark their domain in spent fuel. the pack dive in their desecrated foxholes, sanctify, crane their necks to the sky   howl and howl

    until jinn come crashing   through atmosphere   raze   cities deserts foxholes   turn hellfire on hellfire, silence all howls.

November 4
9:02 p.m.

ix.

    they condensed slogans in pressure cookers

    stuffed them into a brass dallah

    forced us all to drink from the same spout.

    how do you tell a gift giver their drink is tainted

    when they hold rhetoric to your head?

    they'd ask us to change our taste buds, swallow this

    quit howling at the moon.

III

Basha Sparrows

Two brown sparrows flit between shelves
lined with boxes
filled with Abido spices.
They chase bulghur wheat
spilling out from torn bags
over the edges
collecting into piles:
they know to filter the stones.

When the store closes,
the Basha Sparrows fly down
to their favourite aisle
where the Raspberry Barbican is in a puddle.
They chirp Nancy Ajram and Fares Karam songs,
and dance dabke until their feet give.

They go home after fajr.
Their nests made from torn newspaper,
in the rafters
are filled with bulghur, pine-nuts,
salted sunflower seeds.

They'll sleep until after noon
until after prayers
when they'll flutter down
dart between shelves
tear apart spice and wheat bags

God Lives in the Gap Between a Horse's Ears

i.
Frail moth wings beat at the window;
you tell me it's a dead person come to visit,
I say it's just a moth.

ii.
We lose ourselves in between monuments
a graveyard comes to life
final rites whispered.

iii.
Birds find their homes
in ancient Petran tombs
the threshold disinvites us.

iv.
In the valley of space
you turn to stardust
catastrophe after catastrophe.

v.
Witness stolen art, wares, culture.
Get robbed in the rain
by a British bike sharing app.

vi.
The step counter in your phone
has never been this proud;
how do you tell it you're going back to sloth?

vii.
They say there is no discernable difference
between horse meat and beef.
I wonder if racehorses taste bitter.

viii.
This sky is scraped blood orange
smoke-tinged summers
forever.

نار ورمان

Baba didn't expect to lose
عينو
when Mama split open
a late season رمان
بالمطبخ

the imported ones you get
من السوبرستور
من والمارت

that sit
because nobody is interested in that war—

I'm told
    that peeling a pomegranate
    is easier
    when you submerge it in water.

I wonder if
hennaing your fingers, hands,
arms crimson
    makes it all that much sweeter—

Mama dusts
رمان
seeds بالملح
stuffs fire down

her throat. Her face contorts, collapses,
before she eats more—

Baba قطف his عين
cleans his eye,
cleans the cavern

45

براسو with a rag
a doctor prescribed for wiping away gunpowder residue left
over

من الحرب

شظايا الرمان اختفت

stained tongues, throats, stomachs, turning

us into
رمانة

Mama prescribes me a rag
orders me to wipe the كونترتوب
clean the detonated juice
leftover seeds,   salt,   shrapnel,

until the counter is no longer

fire.

Sesame Love

I meander through the aisles of the overpriced grocery store
across from the gelato shop, because today, I'm too lazy to drive
the twenty minutes through traffic to get to the Middle Eastern
supermarket—
I opt to spend the cash on produce labeled "local," "superfoods,"
"organic."

      And I'm stopped short behind a couple
      eyeing the selection of hummus crowding the end of a fridge
      as they hum and haw at the flavours: Chocolate, Salsa verde,
      Avocado, Pumpkin spice
      and I think, *even the canned shit would taste better than this.*

[in my mother's kitchen, the food processor spins,
      whipped into zealous frenzy, the blades slicing through
ingredients
      creating (now) gentrified food
      into something comprehensible]

The question of "when did *hummus* become hummus" stirs in my head.
      What singular moment in time did the cultural lexicon decide
      this word is acceptable not to italicize. Does the OED have
jurisdiction
      over what is acceptable, or maybe Merriam's Websters, or
maybe Joe
      Biden co-opting the word "inshAllah" in his debate with Trump
      only to sign off on Palestinian genocide a few years later.

The couple single out the Salsa verde or the Avocado or the Chocolate,
as their favourite, noting that sabra does a good job with flavour
balancing.

[the food processor in my mother's kitchen whines
       as it churns chickpeas, t7eene, garlic, salt, olive oil-lemon
       into a perfect spread leaving the kitchen smelling of sesame
       until the next bleaching]

At the checkout counter, the couple's groceries slide down the conveyer belt:
       local, organic fruits and vegetables hide beneath reusable bags
       followed by bottle of kombucha
       veggies patties and tofu wrapped in plastic
       with pita bread supplied by a Lebanese bakery
       and atop the mound, packaged sabra hummus.

And I don't lay the blame at their feet, or in their hands, or on their tastebuds.

Death Attends the عزاء

not to pluck another life
or judge your décor in the living room cabinets—
ones filled with "antique" flintlock guns and crystals
and your uncle's sculptures from the 90s.

Death waits off to the side
sitting near the TV which is set to Al Jazeera—
except for that one time your uncle and you watched *Rat Race* together
and told you not to look during the scene when a character flashes their chest at another
but you look on anyway—

you drink ahwe saada—
chase it down with lukewarm water
leftover date stuffed maamoul from Eid
mixes with graveyard dirt clinging to your fingers
counteract bitterness

with stories. How your grandfather fought
everyone
to leave the hospital
to die with his birds
ones he hunted, bred, and kept on the roof.

Chase stories with memories with spiced rice, meat,
served on century-old chipped plates—
stay until dessert is served, stay until Death is full,
until fajr is called
until the stories tire   —if they can even tire—
there's always more.

We Stop to Imagine a Skyline Without the Fire Stack
For Asma A.

We jaywalk to Safeway
to restock Fuji apples
praying, promising one another,
this time
we'll finish them before they rot.

In the storm drain meant for
thunder showers, small sticks, spent motor oil,
you notice "I ♥ Canada Oil & Gas" stickers
peeled away from bumpers, McDonald's drive thru windows,
microplastics never tasted this good.

We switched to reusables
after plastic bags were phased out;
we forget them anyway.
We bag Fuji apples in plastic.
Now they charge for paper:
    "How many bags do you need?"
    "Zero."

We save thirty cents at the self-checkout,
jaywalk to DQ for Dilly Bars, a Blizzard.
We sit on the patio, eat ice cream, bask in the
reflection of the fire stack, watch ice cream wrappers
caught in winds dance in the parking lot
destined for storm drains.
And we notice
DQ ice cream melts a lot faster
than it used to.

Cosmo? Or Lessons in Cultural Un-Communication

The Bedouin girl leads her flock of sheep/goats
in the rocky Petra hills
barefoot.

The American tourists in the Mövenpick lounge
dress like off-duty US marines stationed in the Middle East:
sand-coloured pants and shirts and steel toe hiking boots

ready to tackle Petra
ready to deploy in the next gulf war
ready to get hustled by locals

and of course, they only speak English
and of course, they expect everyone else to only speak   English
and of course, they get angry when everyone else doesn't speak
English.

~~

You ask for a cosmo
while your husband scrolls through his phone
and the waiter hovers over you wondering what a cosmo is
or what you're asking for.

You ask for a
cosmo.

You ask for a
cos-mo
                      polytan.

A cooooos   mooow?

Acosmo!

Cos   Mo,

until you give up
strut across the lounge
ask the bartender instead.

Origin Myths or A Poem for Survivor's Guilt—Cut Up
For Dr. Kaitlyn P

Indeed, the absence of life of any kind:
no deer, no bears, not even a fox or a timber wolf
brought little lady snail and high-flying duck.

Father could not speak;
an inheritance:
repeated winter on a silver dish.

Our sight improved to the west.

The young ones were never boiled or laid on silver dishes.

And they concluded all people in the world were dead.

ذبيحة or قربان or Your First Beheading Video—Part II

Among one of my father's favourite cliches are:
    if you have nothing to hide, you have nothing to fear.

        I'm told that in an airport setting
        I have "no rights."

I'm not sure how that works exactly
or who came up with the saying,
how it proliferated, but do my rights disappear
when I step into the airport, through revolving glass doors,
a border signalling
no rights vs. rights

        or after check-in, when the person manning the desk
        lets my *just* overweight baggage filled with an extra bag
        of Hershey's Chipits from Costco through?
            Or, it's at security, where they brush my laptop
            with the magic wand expecting to find
gunpowder or cocaine.

At duty-free
        I stop to look at snacks I should have bought outside.
        The air is perfumed with Louis Vuitton,
        someone's father over-sprayed.

        But maybe that's where you lose the right to a free market
        where you're gouged for the smallest bag of M&Ms because
        what other choice do you have?

Or maybe it's in the interrogation room at the DXB airport
after a trip to Turkey in 2014 when people were "joining" ISIS.
Or at the Vancouver airport, being asked by the VPD cop if
my brother and me had bazookas in our luggage.

      Would joking about bazookas been okay for a couple of teens
   lulled into a false sense of security by a jokey cop?
         The K-9 German Shepherd pacing up and down the
walkway
        her handler in tow looking like they were ready for
anything:
            imaginary bazookas, imaginary ISIS affiliates,
imaginary
                 rights.

Immigrant Father Horticulture

I don't remember dandelion heads
or blades of grass
shooting upwards from beneath
black earth or brown earth
crowding radishes and carrots

    you tell me

all I need is manure soil شتل or seeds if I like
                plant
                insha'Allah until harvest

Acknowledgements

The epigraph by Qurait bin Aneef Al-Tamimi is from his poem "لو كنت من مازن".

The epigraph by Mukoma Wa Ngugi is from his poem "Preface: Hunting Words with My Father" from his book *Logotherapy* (University of Nebraska Press, 2016). Used with permission.

"Basha Sparrows" appeared in *CV2* 45:4, Spring 2023. "نار ورمان," "This Sweet Rupture," and "Lebanese Zaatar Mix" appeared in *The Polyglot* Issue #11. My sincere thanks to the editors there for choosing and championing my work.

Versions of some of these poems were previously collected in my chapbook *Sesame Love* from Moon Jelly House. Great thanks to Nisha Patel, Matthew James Wiegel, and Katherine Abbas. The YEG writing community will always have a special place in my heart.

To everyone at University of Alberta Press: thank you for giving this book a home.

To my editor, Kimmy Beach: thank you for your guidance, help, and for making this collection shine.

A special thanks to all the friends I've made at University of Calgary and York University throughout my PhD and MA journeys. The writing communities in Alberta, Ontario, and B.C. have been a blessing to my practice. A particular thank you to Cristalle Smith, Marc Lynch, Dr. Kaitlyn Purcell, and Dania Idriss for their constant and unflinching support.

To my family especially.

To Asma.

Thank you.